SCARRED FOR LIFE

E. WHITNEY CLINE

SCARRED FOR LIFE

E. WHITNEY CLINE

For anyone stitched together and still standing.

TABLE OF CONTENTS

UNCOVERED
PART I

WHY READERS LOVE SCARRED FOR LIFE

Survival is difficult, and this collection of poetry reminds us again and again that we must not turn away. The language of this collection is intensely sensory: heat, teeth, and bruises ground abstract questions about religion, love, and the afterlife in a bodied experience.

—ELISE P., DOCTORAL CANDIDATE,
ENGLISH LITERATURE

E's debut collection hits close to home for anyone who has skinned a knee or two and lived to tell the tale. Her honest look at how moments both big and small make and break us manages to feel both refreshing and familiar, connecting us all with dense tissue that proves we were once here, and we have something to say about it.

—CB WOODS, AUTHOR OF *RIFT*

SCARRED FOR LIFE

there's a scar on my hip
from when they cut
my childhood skin
with a scalpel.
twelve thousand days
have come and gone since then
and the scar aches sometimes.
so i went to a doctor who said,
'you'll always be bruised on the inside.'

how true that is, i thought.
it reminded me of the other scars.
the ones you can't see,
but they ache just the same
and it made sense.

i'm bruised on the inside.

bruised from the poignant traumas
that sliced me wide open.
bruised in my heart and my bones
from when my father left
like his father did.
bruised from my mother's
many silver-tongued lashings.

then there are the bruises
from loves lost,
from ego deaths,
from drug binges,
and the songs i can't listen to anymore
because it will always be too soon.

and the grief—
my god, the grief.

they're all over.
emotional wounds my soul licked clean,
some taking years to mend
while others are freshly black and blue,
their sutures tender to the thought.

but i don't hide the scars or bruises
under long sleeves and sunglasses.
i don't make up tales to explain away my life.
i'll never slather on the oils or the creams
everyone says will make them disappear.
what a tragedy it would be
to erase everything i've survived.

instead, i carry on
and let them burn and breathe,
hoping one day the fresh air
will ease the familiar pangs.
still, i will never be unscarred.

and even when the scars
have healed and faded with time,
they will leave a reminder—the ache.

because, after all,
i'll always be bruised on the inside.

QUIET I LOVE YOUS

not all the memories are bad.

there was this stool.
painted yellow, worn to hell.
a household staple,
perfect for top-shelf retrievals,
like the glassware you take out
only when company comes.
sturdy, chipped at the edges,
but small enough to claim as my own.

i'd drag the stool across the kitchen floor,
its legs squealing a little protest
as it scraped the linoleum
on the way to where my mother sat—
phone pressed to her ear,
voice lilting and alive.

i'd perch beside her,
tugging at the spiral landline cord
that hung like a slinky between worlds.

twist. stretch. wrap. pull. repeat.

sometimes i'd pull it close
and let my eyes go soft,
creating two cords.
a small magic;
a secret between me and physics.

when i got carried away,
mother would snap her fingers once—
a small crack of thunder—
or murmur my name
in that low tone meant just for children,
the kind that warned enough
without breaking rhythm.

i'd stop.
always.
or else.

fear and love were neighbors then,
sharing a thin wall.
but even though her voice
rattled my four-year-old heart,
i'd rest my head in her lap
and wait for her hand—
the gentle weight of it
circling my scalp,
telling me i was safe;
telling me, in that moment
i belonged with her.

now, as a mother myself,
i understand the weariness;
the sharp edge of lost patience,
how love can live inside exhaustion
and still be love.
in another vein, though,
lost patience never excuses
an iron fist on a child's face.

i do know i was always loved, though—
even when it didn't feel that way.

the anger and fear
often echoed louder than i love you,
but i know love was there too—
in the head rubs
and the quiet gestures—
perhaps not always aloud,
but they mattered just the same.

THE SOUND OF SHOWING UP

he scored my childhood
in open chords—
his guitar the soundtrack
of every ordinary morning
and every hard night.

i once heard someone say
eighty percent of being a parent
is simply showing up—
and he arrived every time,
without hesitation,
a steady presence
tuning the air around us.

through small moments,
he instilled quiet lessons
slipped between melodies
and the discipline
from someone who understood
that love is not always easy.

and even in the years
when my resistance tried
to drown out his guidance,
i never reached for that brutal line
kids say when they want to cut deep—
you're not my dad.

because some truths
were already settled in me:
he was my dad.
in every way that mattered.

so this is my belated recognition,
my gratitude for the man
who always showed up—
guitar in hand—
and became the father
he knew i needed.

LET ME GROW YOUNG

i want to chase hours
with my friends,
to build something pointless,
made of sticks and pinecones,
and call it a discovery.

i want curiosity to be
my only concern.
i want to interrogate the world
until language gives up on me.
i want to ask *why*
with every single breath.

i want to speak my wants aloud—
unpolished and unfiltered—
no shadow of punishment
or tremor of being misunderstood.

and when i make mistakes,
let them come,
the small consequences.
they pale beside the grown-up ones
we call responsibilities.

i'm tired of bargaining with minutes,
earning my crumbs,
practicing weather talk in chains
and the schoolyard exchange,
living in a pantomime of connection
beneath fluorescent skies.

when i watch my son—
face smudged with blue ink,
eyes bright with unreason—
i remember that wonder
isn't something you outgrow,
but something you forget,
in all the complexities of life,
even exists.

being young felt unbearable once—
the rules, the reach,
the endless waiting to be
older, bigger, freer.
i didn't know then
that freedom comes dressed
in fake smiles and invoices,
and the view from up here
is actually quite lonely.

but the beauty was in
the unknowing,
in believing the world
was mostly a good place,
in mornings always meaning
a fresh start.

if i could go back,
i'd tell my tender self,
it's ok to be young.
don't do things too fast.
stay here a while.
linger a little longer
in the miracle of not yet.

so when i grow old,
please let me grow young.

give me scraped knees,
give me unmade plans.

give me the ache of not knowing
what i now understand too well:

childhood is not small,
but a gift that disappears
before you even know how to miss it.

HELIOTROPE

my son brought home a cup
with seeds and soil.
he announced
'this will be a sunflower.'
we put it in the window
gave it some water
and today
there was a sprout.

i thought about back then.
when i was just a sprout
reaching for the sun.
i wonder if perhaps
in a parallel somewhere
i'm a sunflower.
i wonder if i bloomed.

maybe tomorrow
i could try
to sprout again.
to maybe even
reach for the sun again.
and maybe if i'm lucky
grow some petals this time.

DEAD DAD CLUB

it was coming,
you'd be going.
life was telling,
time was slowing.

you knew, but you kept,
just a few seconds lost,
some here and some there
and then all at once.

how did when become now?
just yesterday we sat
in bright orange chairs
and i unpacked
the ten-ton suitcase
that i've dragged
for thirty-one years
to hell and then back.

shook voice
and a jittered heart,
weighted words
made a heavy start.
i chugged up a hill
and uncovered scars.
you recognized mine
because they were ours.

my wounds were speaking
so i forgot asking
and asking drifted away.
then asking
was thinking
and thinking
was wondering
and wondering
washed down my face.

when you left
your why went with you,
but i didn't know
i needed it.
now my why
lives behind my eyes
that everyone says
look like yours did.

BEREAVEMENT IS SERVED

first, preheat the past
gather all the now
then, measure what wasn't
and all that should have been.

chop up six long days
mince into the night
combine them with the time
that you'll never get again.

now, prepare the good parts
next, add in the bad
mix it all together
and really stir the ache.

strain your grief today
then, layer it tomorrow
repeat this step forever
then, pour.
then, fold.
then, bake.

A PULSE BETWEEN

when my father died,
his bible came home to me,
wrapped in the hush of his end,
its cover cracked,
the red ribbon resting
on psalm 23.

he was a man of faith,
the lord, his shepherd,
and he was walking
the valley of the shadow,
half in this world,
half in whatever waits beyond.

i realized he was afraid.
the page remembered
where his hand had steadied,
and i imagined him whispering

to a god i've never known.

i don't pray,
but when i touched the ribbon,
my heart broke with hope,
as if belief itself
was a current flowing
through my bones.

my god is the universe
and it's older than faith,
assuring me love is the gravity
that keeps the departed near.

i like to think that, one day,
when i dissolve
into the same hum,
i'll find him there—
not heaven,
but a pulse between planes,
where every question
finally has an answer.

SHARED

THE FIRST CUT

the dark of that night
after you left
i cried in the driveway
i'll never forget

i called you up
you met me outside
and said it was over
a piece of me died

you were the one
at just seventeen
unjaded hearts
a teenage dream

never meant to last
it's not who we were
so painfully young

so beautifully pure

twenty years past
it's been so long
and i still remember
our favorite song

i'm married now but
i still have the box
with the mixtape you made
closeted, locked

i'd love to go back
(though time won't allow)
i wish i knew then
all the things i know now

i guess that's the risk
when the door closes shut
on your first real love
the deepest of cuts

so all i will say with
the greatest of ease
is thank you for
the memories

I ONLY MISSED YOU ONCE

the truth is,
i had already done
all of the unlearning
and untangling
and unloving of you
long before our
final goodbye.

the truth is,
we never fit quite right.
forever fighting to survive
the scorching heat
in a house made of ice,
melting away like the witch
from that movie.

the truth is,
i knew it was over
the night you let
miles of hot concrete
pass under my bare feet.
you didn't notice i was gone
and i didn't miss you.

the truth is,
the next day
when i spit the daggers
from my throat
and watched as they
stuck in your chest,
telling you to leave
and never come back,
i meant it.

until later,
when i heard
someone at the door
and you weren't there.
the truth is,
that's when
i missed you.

because the truth is,
in all the years
i'd spent as an adult,
i never outgrew
the little girl
who was too scared to
see who knocked.

and the truth is,
i'm grateful for
you always knowing
that was your job.

UNTIL THEN

you asked once
if we would ever
meet again.
the answer is yes.
on the day the sun
forgets to rise,
i'll be waiting.
when god herself
appears before me
in the flesh,
call my name and
i'll come running.

THE BURN OF RAGE

we sit across from one another,
talking about the heat,
as if the world isn't burning.
we pretend the ground beneath us
isn't singed with implication.

but there is a flame
behind my teeth.
every word i don't speak
tastes of charcoal.

i thought we were chopped
from the same grain.
i thought our hearts ignited
with the same righteousness.

i play along, nodding
and calling it grace,

though it feels more
like self-immolation.

i've learned that
it's your indifference
which fuels my fury,
a match i must wield carefully
so as not to set you alight.

instead, i swallow fire
and feel the burn of rage,
wondering how long
until i turn to smoke.

DETACHED AT THE HIP

i never thought i'd mourn
a hip i never owned
until our hinge slipped apart
leaving only grinding bone

CHOSEN

you answer my calls,
cradle my secrets,
and stay by my side
out of heart, not obligation.
sometimes love isn't a kiss,
but a hand.
sometimes family isn't given,
but chosen.
and when i chose you,
it was the wisest choice
i've ever made.

WHEN YOU KNOW

when i met you,
the search finally stilled,
and the compass settled.
a sudden certainty,
the truth behind
when you know, you know
was clear:
it simply means,
you've made it home.

LUCKY STARS

one clear aries night,
hydrogen and helium clouds
ignited in nuclear fusion,
formulating to become
the core of a new universe.

the lovers, meant to be—
wrapped in suns and moons
and risings—exploded into
ecliptic constellations.

two celestial bodies—
kois meeting creton; fish and bull—
revolved around one another,
weaving through rows and rows
of magical matter.

trillions of miles away,

venus became mars.
milky way, andromeda;
the perfect alchemy,
occurring in an instant.

and the myths,
light-years behind,
envied such grand timing.

i really don't know
the first thing
about stars.

but i knew in that moment—
over a single hello—
somewhere in the sky,
ours aligned.

FOUND

twenty-nine years
i wandered around
looking for you.

what i didn't know was
in finding you
i'd find myself too.

HOLY THRONE

you fell to your knees,
confessed your worship,
and offered me a ring.

crown in hand,
you named me queen,
and asked to be my king.

we sang our praises,
sealed the promise,
and claimed it as our own.

within these walls
lies a sacred palace,
our gilded holy throne.

THIS IS SO US

A HAIKU

after a long day,
you kiss me, 'hi, how are you?'
'better now,' i say.

SOFT

MY SON, MY SUN

you rose, and the world changed color.
the dark corners softened,
and even the air seemed
to sing your name.
they say your child is your heart
set loose in the world,
but you are more than that.

you are the center i circle
without question.
you are heat and gravity,
the steady burn that keeps the cold
from closing in.
each day you rise brighter—
four years of radiance,
of laughter that splits the dark wide open.

your questions beam across the room,
chasing away what lingers
in the shadows.
even your sadness glows—
soft, golden, honest.
it teaches me that light can ache
and still be light.

i used to crave stillness,
but stillness is what happens
when the sun goes down,
and i never want that quiet again.

if you ever dimmed,
i would not ask you to burn brighter—
only to rest, knowing i'd be there,
a small planet waiting for your return.

you are the day that remade me,
the warmth that keeps my heart
from hardening,
the reason i rise
even when i am tired.

my son, my sun.

HAIR

it used to drive me
up the wall
his busy baby hands
tugging on my hair all night
pulling at the strands

beginning in the early days
just staring at the clock
he'd finally sleep
with his tiny fist
clutched around my locks

this went for years
but now he likes
to smell my hair instead
he holds me close
in the nightlight glow
half asleep in bed

i realized
he wants me near
my anger started waning
his little obsession
a constant connection
and so i stopped complaining

then something strange
i began to love
the closeness in the night
his call for me
my run to him
i've let go of the fight

bedtime dread
is a thing of the past
my curls are growing out
to make them easy
for him to find
and mess them all about

now every evening
i take out the tie
and let my hair hang long
reminding myself
'enjoy this time, you'll miss it
when it's gone'

THE GREATEST VIEW

my sweetest boy, i am always looking.
you don't notice because you're busy
perfecting the creation
or practicing the trick
you want to share with me.
but when you shout, 'mama, look!'
with all the want in the world,
you can trust i've already seen it.
i was looking at you long before your demand.

MIDNIGHT SEARCH BAR

A HAIKU

how to raise a kid
when you're still figuring out
how to raise yourself

NO RESULTS FOUND

A HAIKU

how to protect your
child's heart from the breaks a
mother cannot fix

SOMEWHERE IN THE MIDDLE

if i could summon one wish
i'd ask my years to loosen their grip
or let me walk backward
as you stride forward
so we could find one another—
for just an hour—
in the center of time.

for a moment, we'd be the same.
your eyes would carry the weight
of all you'd learned
and mine would still be soft
with beginnings and firsts
and unknowns.

i would finally understand
what you meant
when you said your pancakes

were too round
and why your socks
were in the lunchbox
next to half-eaten apple slices.
and you would know
that i don't resist your growing
because i doubt you
but because i fear the aches ahead,
the sorrows i'll have to cradle as
you learn to mend them without me.

when the hour had passed,
you'd ascend further into age
while i dissolved back into youth,
perhaps making better choices
this time around—but that could mean
i'd never have you,
so i'd make them all just the same.
we'd echo ourselves back
to floating on opposite currents,
once again misunderstood,
but never forgetting the hour when
our ships met somewhere
in the middle of a temporal ocean.

MAMA BIRD

a bird's heart swells and breaks.

with gratitude
for another day
watching her baby emerge
from their shell.

with wisdom
that every moment
is one closer
to when they fly away.

A MOTHER'S NOTE-TO-SELF

remember:
you were yours
before you were theirs.

COLLECTIVE

WE THE PEOPLE

we the people will throw flames
and coat our bodies in soot,

gather the charred remains and
create the good for the many.

when it's mended, we'll have
something for everyone,
never everything for someone.

THE CIRCUS

a clown with bloody hands
giggles in the stands,
while the ringmaster
whips lions as a game.

the lions maul the clown and say,
'look who's laughing now.
you should have known that
lions can't be tamed.'

FREEDOM RINGS

what goes up
must come down
let's watch it crumble
let's dance on the rubble

FOUNDING MOTHERS

imagine the country mothered
by bodies that know blood,
not from battlefields,
but from crimson tides
that arrive uninvited,
and we politely lay out
an extra place setting.

picture treaties drafted,
between pta meetings
and screaming toddlers
who pull hair for sport,
but our lips remain smiling,
the color unsmudged.

there'd be no declarations signed
next to the smoke of rifles,
only policies braided like hair,

tight, to stay held,
but not enough to strangle.

our groceries are heavy—
milk, tampons, and freedom—
but we lead the charge
with fractured spines.
we've no need to pen bills,
as, here, we honor
your god-given rights
upon the moment you emerge from within.

empires are built on empathy,
not ammunition;
nations in careful hands,
not on necks.
we'd stockpile compassion,
not bombs,
and balance the budget
without breaking a sweat.

we'd burn this one down
and start over fresh.
the american dream is
a nightmare anyway,
save for the ones who
purchase prestige with
dirty dollars or
occupy egos so phallic
they deflate in the

absence of adoration.

it should have been
the founding mothers.
our new world would've stood
how our children do—
upright, strong, and
brimming with possibilities—
rather than smeared under
perspirant men like a
certain shade of sprayed-on tan.

those dreadful fore fathers
founded nothing.
they played finders' keepers—
a child's game of take—
then carved their
signatures in stone,
while mothers' backs shattered
beneath the burden.

and yet, the mothers go unnamed.

FUCK ICE

they promised
american dreams
and all we got
were night terrors

INFERNO

the olive-skinned children,
with charred organs
under smoky skies,
have turned my heart to ash.

i wish for endings
amongst the pyre
of soulless bodies
engulfed in silent luxury.
yet the only thing to come
from my dreaming
is the heat of the truth.

one day,
when the child burns
on your doorstep,
you'll swear you've been
shouting fire.
but today,
it's not your house
so you pretend not to see
the flames.

THE PALESTINIAN MOTHER

there is no difference, mother,
between myself
and the palestinian woman
who created bones and laughter
with her magical body
to become a mother.
the way i did.
the way you did, mother.

the same woman
who then held
and rocked
and whispered
endless goodbyes
to the skin of her skin,
the heart of her heart,
and cradled him close
as he lay in a bag.

i will think of her
every day, mother.
how can i not
summon myself, mother?
how can i not speak
for the ones
kissing their children
through blood-stained cloths?

and if you are not called
to move the earth, mother,
to protect every child, mother—
to protect every child's mother—
then how, mother,
do you dare
call yourself 'mother?'

SHE

a woman is scorned
her girdle is torn
locked in a kitchen
always tending to him
she wants nothing except
the rights he has and yet
he takes everything from her
limb to limb

she bears life like a god
so she finds it odd
that he claims
her body his to keep
reduced and hidden
to question is forbidden
she sits in silence
but her mind never sleeps

more powerful than he
she is not cut
still she bleeds
while taking care
of everyone around
through her gritted teeth
she asks him what he needs
with wrists tied
her legs tightly bound

she formulates her plan
a fuck you to his clan
the fight to take back
what is rightfully hers
she will do it all
cannot wait to watch him fall
and upon him she will cast
a woman's curse

then the day arrives
and the patriarchy dies
he declares 'but i am the man'
she looks into his eyes
slits his throat and when he cries
she gets close and says
'not half the man i am'

RUNNERS

we are the runners
who built the path—
straight forward,
in an orderly fashion—
our footsteps the labor
of a road that leads to nothing.

we run in place
toward an illusory somewhere
on a treadmill older than dreams.
the belt whispers faster,
while the horizon sits perfectly still—
a distant finish line never crossed.

they tell us it's the way, so we run.
stopping feels like failure, so we run.
nothing turns without us, so we run.
and those above the track

pretend they bore our legs.

they've poisoned the water
our parched tongues beg to drink.
exhausted by the chase,
we reach for everything
they'll never let us hold.

but even in the sprint,
there's a soft, stubborn hope
beneath our feet:
if every tired runner
stepped off at once,
we'd shift the entire world.

so we have to believe
that we, the runners,
could one day change course,
could one day slow down,
could one day rest,
and still win the race
together.

UNCOVERED
PART II

BONES

every day
she breaks the bones
a little more.

that's what happens
when you build a house
on skeletons.

THE TORNADO

the tornado arrived smiling,
looking for something to destroy,
with a wind so sharp
it cut roofs from their beams,
and turned the sky
a warning shade of green.

i was a small town then,
easy for the funnel to swallow
and twist through streets,
lifting truths from their foundations,
ripping me from my mother,
our home split clean in two.

no longer small,
i grew into a city,
steel-spined and harder to shake,
but still pocketed with ruins—
leveled lots where trust once stood,
sidewalks cracked from the
weight of secrets,
the quiet knowledge that
i can never fully reclaim
what the storm stripped away.

the thunder may have silenced,
but its memory echoes now,
not against my skyline,
but in the stories told
of a small town wrecked
by a great tornado.

PAST MEETS PRESENT

past, present.
present, past.

they shake hands.

past goes in for a hug.

present says,
'i've heard so much about you.'

past, a musty brown carpet,
the door that never closed right,
shadows dancing in the hall.

present, white sheets soaked
in the sweat of regret.

they huddle close
and so begins the undoing.

past rips the seams;
a four-year-old backhanded
in the front seat
of a blue corolla.

present threads a needle;
jokes over scrambled eggs
and french toast.

the shredded linens,
a heap on the floor.
no one sleeps.

the sun is full of hope,
but the moon
watched the battle.

past mourns the morning.
present is heavy and heaving.

past drinks orange juice.
present adds vodka.
it's quiet now.

dark rounds the sky again.

past makes an entrance.
present rolls her eyes.

they embrace and pick up
where they left off.

THE DOOR

a door is a curious thing.
it keeps us in
while keeping us out—
a paradox of passage.
how can two truths
exist at once?
how can a body
be both the keeper
and the kept?
i've stood here all this time,
two versions of myself,
each as steadfast
and unwilling to
make the first move
as the other.

i've been living in the hush
behind this swollen door,

its chocolate hinges addled
with unshed words.
it knows the swirls
of my fingertips by heart.
it knows the ache
of wanting out.

i've traced the wood's grain
a million times
like scripture;
counted each splinter
as remorse;
the knob forever a hazy sun
i'd orbit but never turn.

i convinced myself
the world was too bright
for what i carry.
so i built a kingdom
out of shadow and repetition,
fed myself silence,
slept beneath the hum
of my own denial.
still, whispers seeped out
from under the cracks—
quiet voices made of marrow
and memories,
saying *open me.*

but fear is fluent

in paralysis.
it knows how to hold you
with your hand on the lever;
it knows how to make stillness
feel like safety.

when at last i moved—
when the latch sighed
and light unspooled itself
across the room—
the air changed shape.

everything i've hidden
tumbled out in a chorus
of confessions—
my dust,
my bones,
my darkness—
all naming me in unison.

but there he stood—
soft as dusk after rain—
and did not turn away.
he breathed compassion
into my wreckage.
he stayed.

now i must learn
how to live in the open,
how to call it by name,

how to trust the sounds
that comes from my throat.

there is no closing it again.
the light cannot unsee.

the door stands,
but no longer keeps me.
it only reminds me
of the weight of silence
and how heavy
a knob can be
when the screws
are caked in rust.

i can see now
that the hardest part
was never in opening the door,
but rather in believing
someone would stay
once they saw
what was on the other side.

DRIVE HOME

i sing
my hymns
so loud
because i
can't bear
to hear
what the
ghosts have
to say

HERE LIES

i was not a saint, but a sentence—
sometimes a run-on, sometimes a fragment—
always searching for a period
that didn't look like an ending,
and a deep love for the aside
of an em dash.

do not dare say i passed away.
instead, say I tripped
and fell headlong into the velvet absurdity of
elsewhere,
where decorum has no dominion,
and even the angels' hair is unkempt.

i was afraid of death—
afraid of silence, afraid of the nothing.
but i was afraid of life too—
afraid of small talk,

afraid of not pressing my words into clay
before the kiln cooled.

so i wrote letters that stammered,
poems that swayed,
epitaphs disguised as love notes
and love notes disguised as apologies.

if you wish to remember me,
remember i worshipped misbehaved scripture,
that i preferred daisies called solar vagabonds
and grief a carnivorous inheritance—
or something equally as infuriatingly beautiful—
by the dickinsons, the plaths, and the bukowskis.
remember i painted my bruises with metaphors,
because plain speech felt too naked.

now i am deliciously unbuttoned.
no obligations or inbox,
no need to tuck in my stomach
or be polite to men who stare.
i lounge in infinity like it's a hammock
strung between unruly stars,
laughing at how much time i wasted
trying to deserve my own air.

if you love me,
set my name loose in prose,
let it mingle with verbs that outpace the grave.
let me stumble,

let me live madly,
the way i never quite dared here.

and when you say goodbye,
say it slant.
say it sideways.
say it the way my son mispronounces spaghetti.
because i am not gone—
i am forever scattered in margins
and unfinished works that still breathe on paper,
the ink smudged with laughter.
i am a chorus of half-formed ideas
just waiting for their moment in the sun.

WHAT A DREAM

i dreamed i turned
my insides outward
and penned something
wide enough to hold
both myself and a stranger
of the same cloth.

i dreamed of my name
inked along a spine,
breathing the same air
as the ones who built
the very bridges i now cross.

i dreamed i rested among them,
collecting dust and light,
until someone came along
and decided i was worth opening.
oh, what a dream.

ACKNOWLEDGEMENTS

Writing these acknowledgments feels surreal. Publishing a book of poetry has been a lifelong dream, and I am so incredibly grateful for the people who helped me get here.

To my husband, Brian: Thank you for your love and genuine enthusiasm for this project. I would be lost without your tolerance of all the late-night writing sessions, and willingness to hear a million versions of the same poem over and over as I reworked every single one. I'm so happy I married you.

To the love of my life, Barrett: You are the best thing that has ever happened to me and my greatest inspiration. I love you bigger than the universe and I always will, no matter what.

To my confidant and partner in delusion, Shelly: I hold our grief-bond-turned-creative-companionship so close to my heart and I hope to know you forever. Thank you for believing in me, thank you for the push, and thank you for saving my sanity more times than I can count. I quite literally could not have done this without you.

To my mom, Linn: I'm sorry for all the times I forgot that, like the rest of us, you're doing life for the first time. Thank you for the love and the lessons. You will always be my mama.

To my chosen father, Mark: There aren't words to fully capture how appreciative I am for your presence in my life. You're the dad I needed and deserved. Thank you for showing up.

To my brother, Drew: You are the reason I started writing. My trauma-bonded role model, thank you for leading the way.

To my dad, Wink: I wish we'd had more time to build what we never got to while you were here. The scars left by your absence—both in life and in death—will never fully heal, but they'll always be a reminder of the unparalleled love I hold for you.

To my dearest friends, Sterling and Amanda: My cheerleaders. My safe places. My number-one fans. I love you.

And to every *Scarred for Life* reader: Thank you for being here and for lending me your time. All I've ever wanted is to inspire through words and, by opening this book, you have healed me in ways I never thought possible. I am profoundly humbled.

ABOUT THE AUTHOR

E. Whitney Cline is a writer, editor, and poet, capturing the highs and lows of the human condition in her first poetry collection, *Scarred For Life*. She is one of the founding members and Editor-in-Chief at Emrae Publishing, a profit-share indie press.

Follow her at @ewhitneycline on Instagram.

EMRAE PUBLISHING

Emrae Publishing challenges traditional and hybrid publishing houses with a profit-share model. With a focus on direct distribution and partnerships with independent bookstores, Emrae gives authors the flexibility of self-publishing with the support of a team that understands them. Their mission is to keep money in the pockets of creatives bringing stories to life while keeping billionaires out of their business.

Discover new voices at reademrae.com